Natural Disasters

Earthquake!

For my grandchildren —M. D. B.

To Isaac's friend Sam —J. G. W.

SIMON SPOTLIGHT
An imprint of Simon & Schuster Children's Publishing Division
1230 Avenue of the Americas, New York, NY 10020
This Simon Spotlight edition December 2019
First Aladdin Paperbacks edition April 2009
Text copyright © 2009 by Marion Dane Bauer
Illustrations copyright © 2009 by John Wallace
SIMON SPOTLIGHT, READY-TO-READ, and colophon are registered
trademarks of Simon & Schuster, Inc.
For information about special discounts for bulk purchases, please
contact Simon & Schuster Special Sales at 1-866-506-1949 or
business@simonandschuster.com.
Manufactured in the United States of America 1019 LAK
2 4 6 8 10 9 7 5 3 1
The Library of Congress has cataloged the paperback edition as follows:
Bauer, Marion Dane.
Earthquake! / by Marion Dane Bauer ; illustrated by John Wallace. —
1st. Aladdin Paperbacks ed.
p. cm. — (Ready-to-read)
1. Earthquakes—Juvenile literature. I. Wallace, John, 1966– ill. II. Title.
QE521.3.B389 2009
551.22—dc22
2008050236
ISBN 978-1-5344-5561-0 (hc)
ISBN 978-1-4169-2551-4 (pbk)

Natural Disasters

Earthquake!

By **Marion Dane Bauer**

Illustrated by **John Wallace**

Ready-to-Read

SIMON SPOTLIGHT
New York London Toronto Sydney New Delhi

Did you know the ground
we stand on is moving
all the time?

Usually it moves as slowly as your fingernails grow.

It moves so slowly,
the ground seems to
be perfectly still.

Sometimes, though, the ground moves suddenly. Then the movement is called an earthquake.

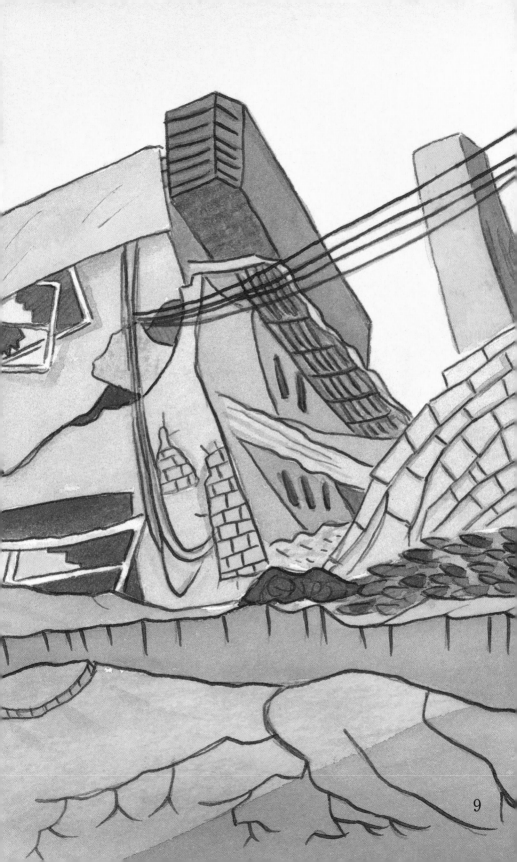

How can the solid
ground quake?

Let us look at the way
our world is made.

The Earth is round like a ball.
Deep inside the Earth is a
core.

The inside of the core
is very hot solid metal.
The outside of the core
is hot liquid metal.

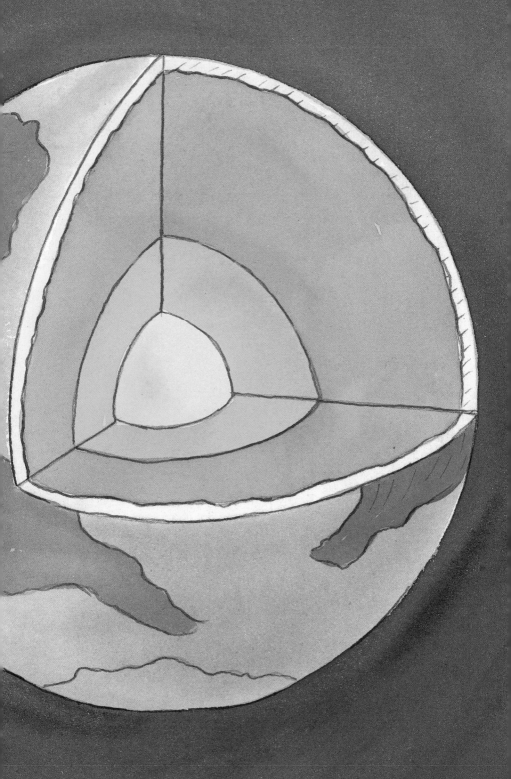

The next layer is
called the mantle.
The mantle is hot too.

It is hot enough for rocks to
ooze like caramel.
On top of the hot rocks
lies the crust.

We live on the crust.

The crust is broken into
plates that fit together
like a jigsaw puzzle.
The plates float on the
hot, oozing rocks.

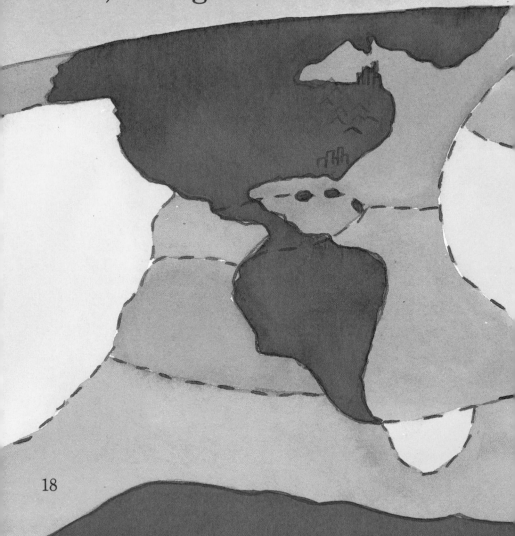

Because the plates float,
the pieces of the puzzle push
against one another
or pull apart.

They push until one plate
suddenly slips sideways.

Or until the two plates bump up against each other.

Or until one plate slides below the other.

That sudden movement is an
earthquake!

Long ago, people made up stories to explain earthquakes.

Some Native Americans
believed the world was held
on the backs of seven turtles.
When the turtles moved—
earthquake!

The Japanese believed a huge
catfish lived deep in the Earth.
When it thrashed about, the
Earth shook.

Some Africans thought
the world was balanced on the
hand of a giant. When the giant
sneezed—earthquake!

Earthquakes are difficult to predict.

Scientists can make an educated guess where an earthquake will happen, but not when.

Earthquakes formed our world.
Earthquakes are changing it
still.

Interesting Facts About Earthquakes

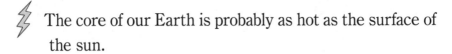 The core of our Earth is probably as hot as the surface of the sun.

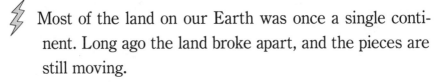 Most of the land on our Earth was once a single continent. Long ago the land broke apart, and the pieces are still moving.

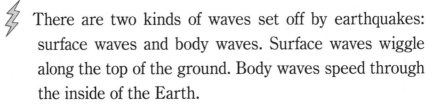 There are two kinds of waves set off by earthquakes: surface waves and body waves. Surface waves wiggle along the top of the ground. Body waves speed through the inside of the Earth.

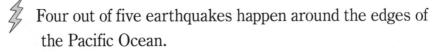 Four out of five earthquakes happen around the edges of the Pacific Ocean.

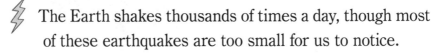 The Earth shakes thousands of times a day, though most of these earthquakes are too small for us to notice.